A LOOK AT US HISTORY

THE ARTICLES OF CONFEDERATION

BY BRAY JACOBSON

Gareth Stevens PUBLISHING

CRASHCOURSE

Please visit our website, www.garethstevens.com. For a free color catalog of all our high-quality books, call toll free 1-800-542-2595 or fax 1-877-542-2596.

Library of Congress Cataloging-in-Publication Data

Names: Jacobson, Bray, author.
Title: The Articles of Confederation / Bray Jacobson.
Description: New York : Gareth Stevens Publishing, 2018. | Series: A look at US history | Includes index.
Identifiers: LCCN 2016037130| ISBN 9781482460353 (pbk. book) | ISBN 9781482460360 (6 pack) | ISBN 9781482460377 (library bound book)
Subjects: LCSH: United States. Articles of Confederation. | Constitutional history--United States--18th century.
Classification: LCC KF4508 .J33 2018 | DDC 342.7302--dc23
LC record available at https://lccn.loc.gov/2016037130

First Edition

Published in 2018 by
Gareth Stevens Publishing
111 East 14th Street, Suite 349
New York, NY 10003

Designer: Samantha DeMartin
Editor: Kristen Nelson

Photo credits: Series art Christophe BOISSON/Shutterstock.com; (feather quill) Galushko Sergey/Shutterstock.com; (parchment) mollicart-design/Shutterstock.com; cover, p. 1 (left article) the government of the United States/Wikimedia Commons; cover, p. 1 (right article) The National Archive/Wikimedia Commons; p. 5 Hulton Archive/Hulton Archive/Getty Images; p. 7 GraphicaArtis/Archive Photos/Getty Images; p. 9 The White House Historical Association/ Wikimedia Commons; pp. 11, 19, 23 (main) courtesy of the Library of Congress; p. 13 New York Public Library/Wikimedia Commons; p. 15 MPI/Archive Photos/Getty Images; p. 17 courtesy of FCIT/ http://etc.usf.edu/maps; p. 21 UniversalImagesGroup/Universal Images Group/Getty Images; p. 23 (inset) U.S. Post Office/Wikimedia Commons; p. 25 kateukraine/ Shutterstock.com; p. 27 Hulton Archive/Archive Photos/Getty Images; p. 29 Bettmann/ Bettmann/Getty Images.

Printed in the United States of America

CPSIA compliance information: Batch #CS17GS: For further information contact Gareth Stevens, New York, New York at 1-800-542-2595.

CONTENTS

Words in the glossary appear in **bold** type the first time they are used in the text.

THE CONGRESSES

In September 1774, the First Continental Congress met in Philadelphia, Pennsylvania. **Representatives** from 12 of the 13 British colonies attended. They wanted more say in government and felt England controlled them too tightly. But the British king paid no attention.

MAKE THE GRADE

In April 1775, the Battles of Lexington and Concord became the first of the American Revolution.

The Second Continental Congress met beginning in May 1775. By then, some representatives wanted to **declare** freedom from England. The idea of joining under one government had been brought up before. Benjamin Franklin had presented one such plan—the Albany Plan—in 1754.

MAKE THE GRADE

The Albany Plan said the colonies would govern themselves, but still answer to the British king.

Second Continental Congress

On July 21, 1775, Franklin introduced a new **document** that would set up an independent government. The congress talked about it—but didn't **ratify** it. Franklin's "Articles of **Confederation** and **Perpetual** Union" was a major step toward the colonies' future government.

Benjamin Franklin

MAKE THE GRADE

During the American Revolution (1775–1783), the Continental Congress was the voice of the colonies to Great Britain. It also served as the government during that time.

THE LEE RESOLUTIION

It wasn't until June 7, 1776, that the congress began to consider another plan for independence. The Lee **Resolution** suggested that three documents be written, including a "plan of confederation." The congress formed a committee, or group, to write this plan.

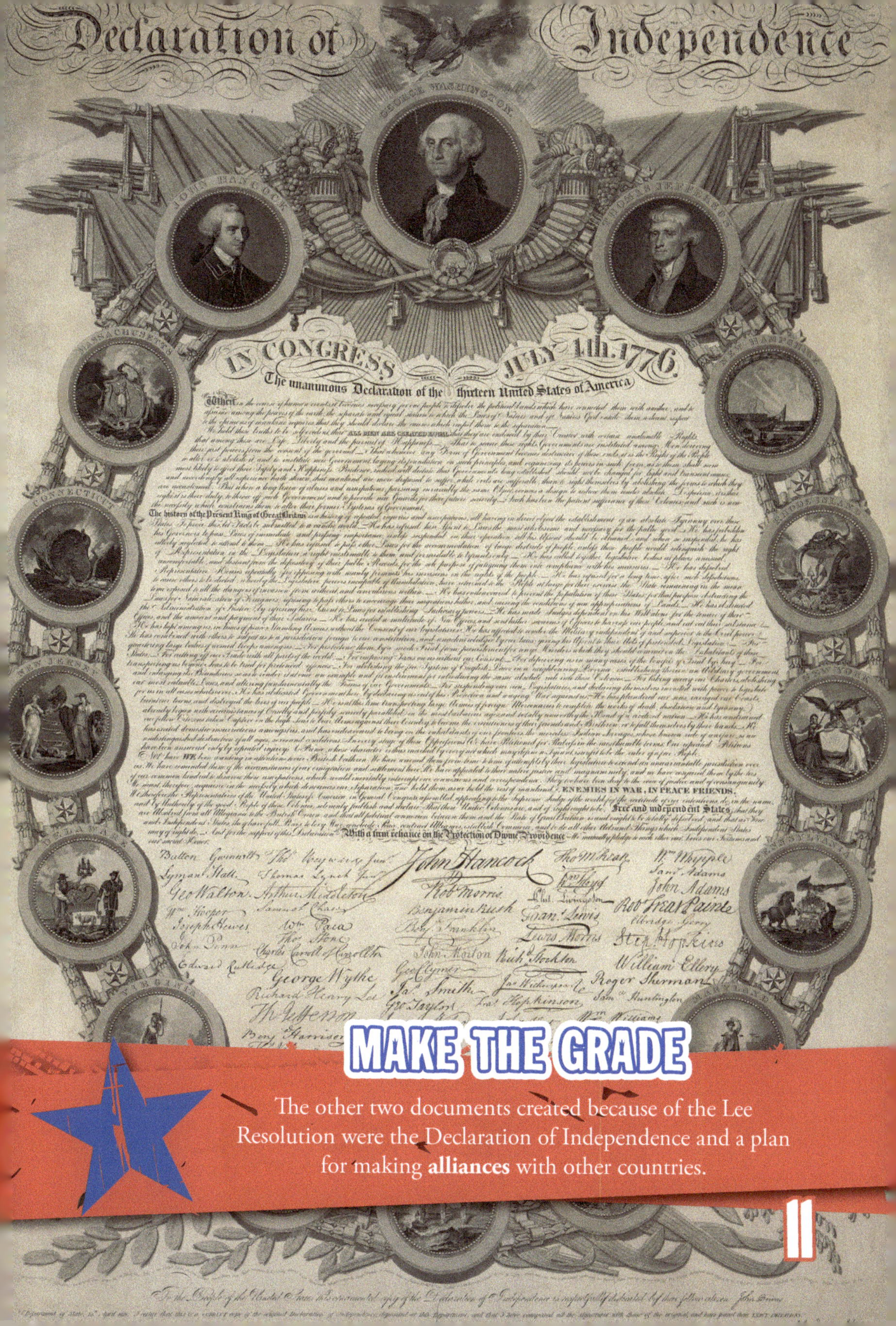

MAKE THE GRADE

The other two documents created because of the Lee Resolution were the Declaration of Independence and a plan for making **alliances** with other countries.

John Dickinson, a representative from Pennsylvania, led the committee working on the plan for confederation. He wrote a **draft** of the Articles of Confederation and presented it to the congress on July 12, 1776. The representatives made many changes.

John Dickinson

MAKE THE GRADE

In the first draft of the Articles, the representatives disagreed on taxes, representation in Congress, and how to deal with western lands.

RATIFIED!

On November 15, 1777, the Articles of Confederation was officially ratified by the congress. Now, all 13 colony-states had to ratify it. Virginia was the first to do so. Maryland was the last, ratifying the document in 1781!

ARTICLES

OF

Confederation

AND

Perpetual Union

BETWEEN THE

STATES

OF

NEW-HAMPSHIRE, MASSACHUSETTS-BAY, RHODE-ISLAND AND PROVIDENCE PLANTATIONS, CONNECTICUT, NEW-YORK, NEW-JERSEY, PENNSYLVANIA, DELAWARE, MARYLAND, VIRGINIA, NORTH-CAROLINA, SOUTH-CAROLINA AND GEORGIA.

MAKE THE GRADE

The biggest change in the final document was that states had more power than the central, or national, government. In the draft, more power was with the central government.

THE ARTICLES

The Articles of Confederation has 13 parts, or articles. The first named the country "the United States." Article 2 made the states free and gave powers not with the central government to them. According to Article 3, the states would unite in the face of an enemy.

MAKE THE GRADE

In Article 4, it's written that everyone living in the United States should be treated fairly, no matter the state they're in.

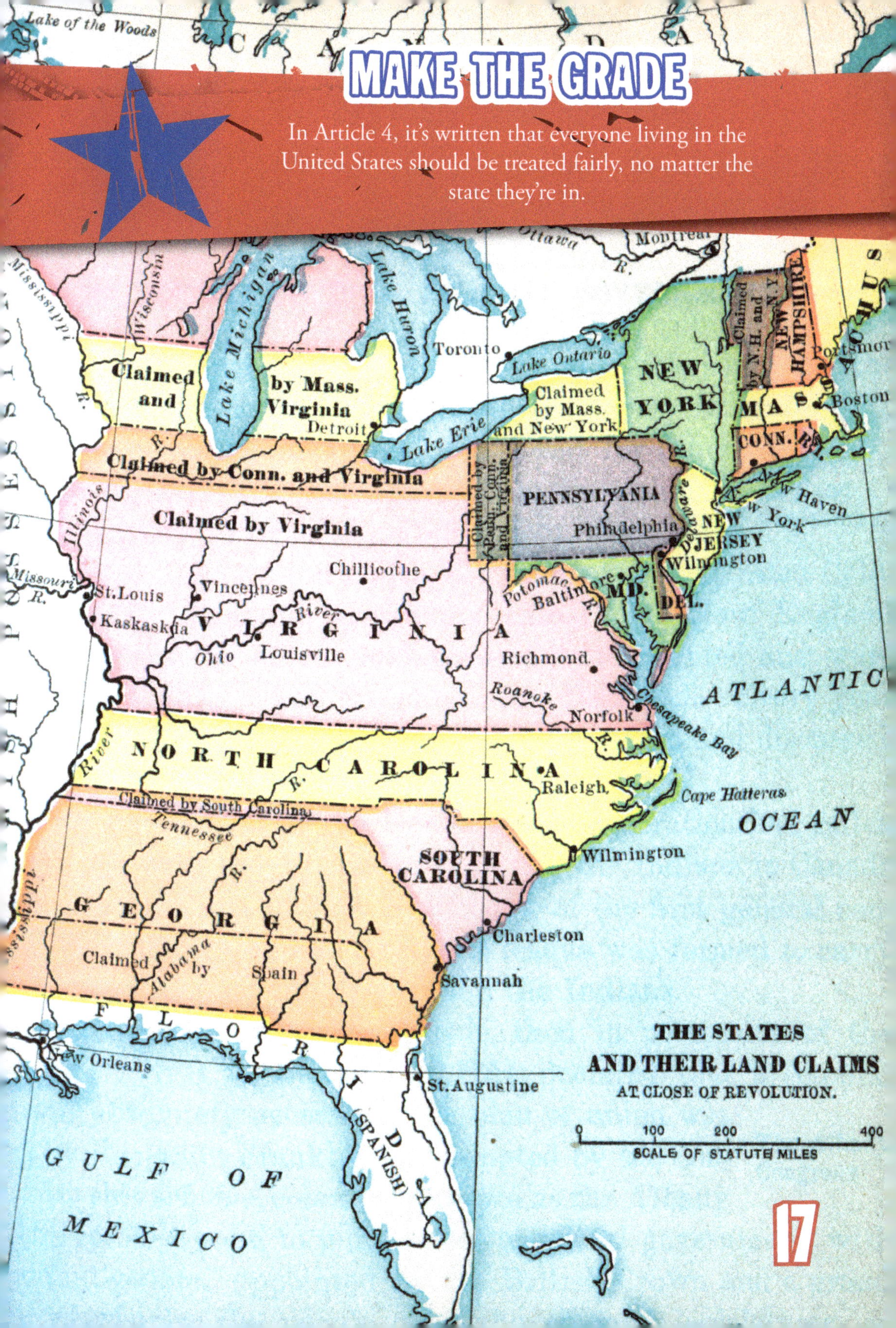

In Article 5, Congress was established. States were given two to seven representatives who were allowed to serve for 3 of every 6 years. The representatives would vote together, giving each state one vote in Congress.

MAKE THE GRADE

Article 9 gave Congress its powers, including declaring war and dealing with disagreements between states.

Full faith and credit ſhall be given in each of theſe ſtates to the records, acts, and judicial proceedings, of the courts and magiſtrates of every other ſtate.

Art. V. For the more convenient management of the general intereſts of the United States, delegates ſhall be annually appointed, in ſuch manner as the legiſlature of each ſtate ſhall direct, to meet in Congreſs on the firſt *Monday* in *November*, in every year, with a power reſerved to each ſtate to recall its delegates, or any of them, at any time within the year, and to ſend others in their ſtead for the remainder of the year.

No ſtate ſhall be repreſented in Congreſs by leſs than two, nor by more than ſeven, members; and no perſon ſhall be capable of being a delegate for more than three years, in any term of ſix years; nor ſhall any perſon, being a delegate, be capable of holding any office under the United States, for which he, or another for his benefit, receives any ſalary, fees, or emolument of any kind.

Each ſtate ſhall maintain its own delegates in a meeting of the ſtates, and while they act as members of the committee of the ſtates.

In determining queſtions in the United States, in Congreſs aſſembled, each ſtate ſhall have one vote.

Freedom of ſpeech and debate in Congreſs ſhall not be impeached or queſtioned in any court, or place, out of Congreſs; and the members of Congreſs ſhall be protected in their perſons from arreſts and impriſonments during the time of their going to and from and attendance on Congreſs, except for treaſon, felony, or breach of the peace.

Art. VI. No ſtate, without the conſent of the United States in Congreſs aſſembled, ſhall

THE STATES

States couldn't form alliances or raise **permanent** armed forces, according to Article 6, though they could have **militias**. Article 7 notes that states could choose some lower militia leaders. Article 8 created a way for the government to make money through state taxes.

MAKE THE GRADE

Article 9 formed a Committee of States. Article 10 said the committee could make decisions with Congress's powers when Congress wasn't meeting.

Article 11 made adding new states possible, if three-quarters of states agreed to it. Article 12 promised that the new country would pay back the money borrowed from other countries before the Articles of Confederation was written.

MAKE THE GRADE

Article 13 declared that the document was the top law of the land, but that it could be changed, or amended, if all states ratified the changes.

on by the United States, in Congreſs aſſembled, [illegible] men, bled, ſhall, on conſideration of circumſtances, ju[illegible] eater or ſhould raiſe a ſmaller number than its quota [illegible] ſhed, number of men than the quota thereof, ſuch e[illegible] ure of armed, and equipped, in the ſame manner as [illegible] which ſuch ſtate ſhall judge that ſuch extra number c[illegible] s they caſe they ſhall raiſe, officer, clothe, arm, an[illegible] pped, judge can be ſafely ſpared. And the officers [illegible] s, in ſhall march to the place appointed, and within [illegible] Congreſs aſſembled.

The United States, in Congreſs aſſembled, [illegible] ters of marque and repriſal, in time of peace, nor enter into any treaties or alliances, [illegible] money, nor regulate the value thereof, nor aſcertain the ſums and expenſes neceſſary for the defence and welfare of the United States, or any of them, nor emit bills, nor borrow money on the credit of the United States, nor appropriate money, nor agree upon the number of veſſels of war to be built or purchaſed, or the number of land or ſea forces to be raiſed, nor appoint a commander in chief of the army or navy, unleſs nine ſtates aſſent to the ſame; nor ſhall a queſtion on any other point, except for adjourning from day to day, be determined, unleſs by the votes of a majority of the United States, in Congreſs aſſembled.

The Congreſs of the United States ſhall have power to adjourn to any time within the year, and to any place within the United States, ſo that no period of adjournment be for a longer duration than the ſpace of ſix months, and ſhall publiſh the journal of their proceedings monthly, except ſuch part thereof relating to treaties, alliances, or military operations, as in their judgment require ſecrecy; and the yeas and nays of the delegates of each ſtate on any queſtion ſhall be entered on the journal, when it is deſired by any delegate; and the delegates of a ſtate, or any of them, at his or their requeſt, ſhall be furniſhed with a tranſcript of the ſaid journal, except ſuch parts as are above excepted, to lay before the legiſlatures of the ſeveral ſtates.

ART. X. The committee of the ſtates, or any nine of them, ſhall be authoriſed to execute, in the receſs of Congreſs, ſuch of the powers of Congreſs as the United States, in Congreſs aſſembled, by the conſent of nine ſtates, ſhall from time to time think expedient to veſt them with; provided, that no power be delegated to the ſaid committee, for the exerciſe of which, by the articles of confederation, the voice of nine ſtates, in the Congreſs of the United States aſſembled, is requiſite.

ART. XI. Canada acceding to this confederation, and joining in the meaſures of the United States, ſhall be admitted into, and entitled to, all the advantages of this union; but no other colony ſhall be admitted into the ſame, unleſs ſuch admiſſion be agreed to by nine ſtates.

ART. XII. All bills of credit emitted, monies borrowed, and debts contracted by or under the authority of Congreſs, before the aſſembling of the United States, in purſuance of the preſent confederation, ſhall be deemed and conſidered as a charge againſt the United States, for payment and ſatisfaction whereof the ſaid United States, and the publick faith, are hereby ſolemnly pledged.

ART. XIII. Every ſtate ſhall abide by the determinations of the United States, in Congreſs aſſembled, on all queſtions which by this confederation are ſubmitted to them. And the articles of this confederation ſhall be inviolably obſerved by every ſtate, and the union ſhall be perpetual; nor ſhall any alteration at any time hereafter be made in any of them, unleſs ſuch alteration be agreed to in a Congreſs of the United States, and be afterwards confirmed by the legiſlatures of every ſtate.

THESE articles ſhall be propoſed to the legiſlatures of all the United States, to be conſidered; and if approved of by them, they are adviſed to authoriſe their delegates to ratify the ſame in the Congreſs of the United States, which [illegible]

ARTICLES IN ACTION

Once the Articles of Confederation united the colonies as states, the new government settled arguments over land in the West. Congress passed the Northwest Ordinance in 1787, which set up how western lands could become states. However, the central government didn't have enough power.

MAKE THE GRADE

The Articles of Confederation gave so much power to the states partly because many colonists felt more loyal to their colony—now state—than the new country.

NORTHWEST TERRITORY 1787

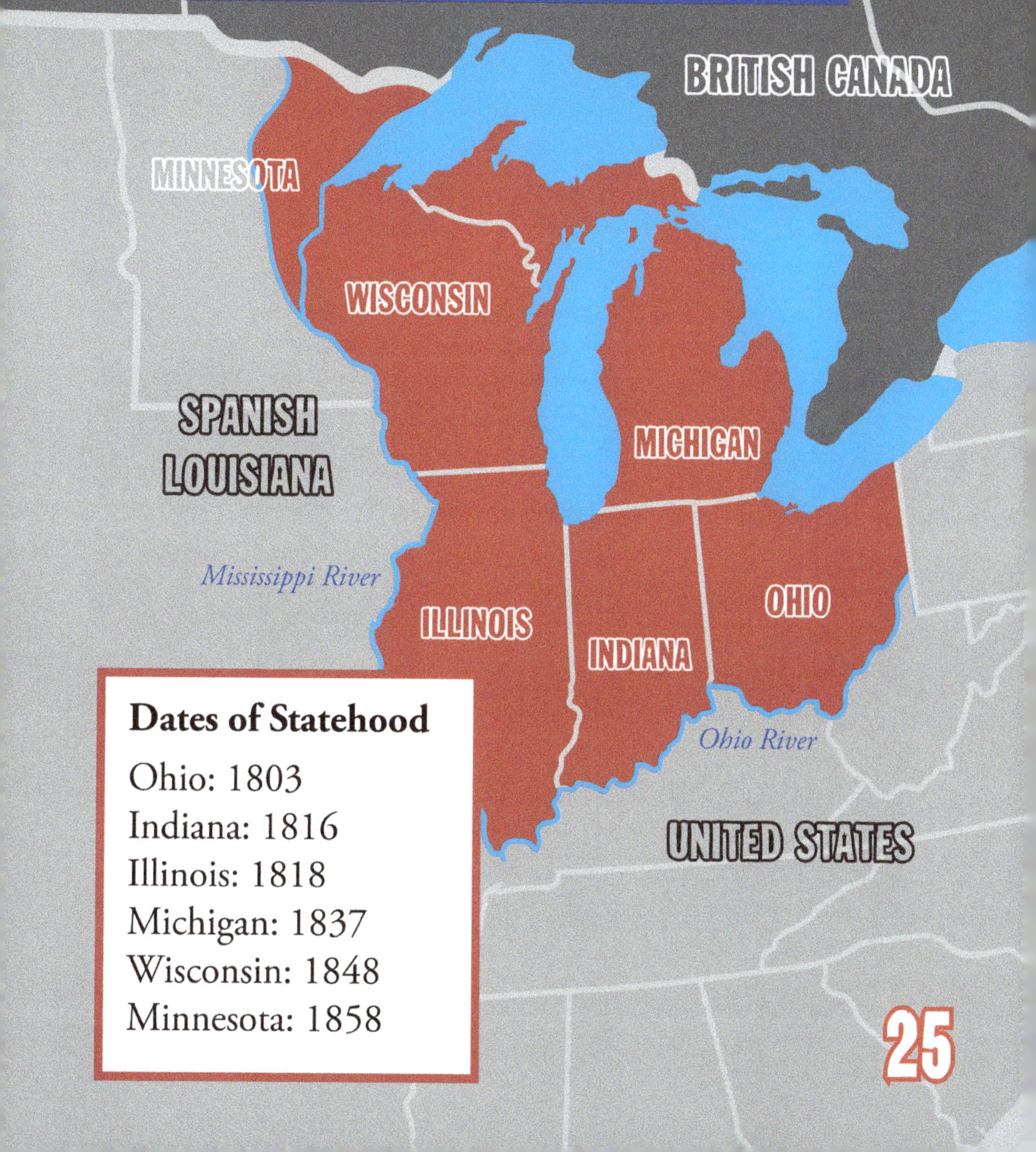

Dates of Statehood

Ohio: 1803
Indiana: 1816
Illinois: 1818
Michigan: 1837
Wisconsin: 1848
Minnesota: 1858

The states often ignored Congress, especially when it came time to pay money owed. Congress was unable to make them give money or troops when needed. So, in 1787, representatives from the states met to work out the Articles' problems.

MAKE THE GRADE

The Massachusetts militia faced uprisings against taxes called Shays's **Rebellion** in 1786 and 1787. The national government wasn't able to help, showing how weak it was.

THE CONVENTION

The representatives soon found that the Articles couldn't be fixed. Instead, their meeting became the Constitutional **Convention**. The US Constitution went into effect on March 4, 1789. Though in use for a short time, the Articles of Confederation was an important step toward today's government!

MAKE THE GRADE

The Constitution gave the central government more power, but still gave all powers not given to the central government to the states.

TIMELINE OF THE ARTICLES OF CONFEDERATION

September 5, 1774
The First Continental Congress begins.

May 5, 1775
The Second Continental Congress begins.

June 7, 1776
The Lee Resolution is introduced.

July 2, 1776
The congress agrees to the Declaration of Independence.

July 12, 1776
The first draft of the Articles of Confederation is brought to the congress.

November 15, 1777
The Articles of Confederation is adopted by the Continental Congress.

March 1, 1781
Maryland is the last state to ratify the Articles.

May 25, 1787
The Constitutional Convention begins.

March 4, 1789
The US Constitution takes the place of the Articles.

GLOSSARY

alliance: an agreement between two or more groups to work together

confederation: a league of people or states that support each other and act together

convention: a gathering of people who have a common interest or purpose

declare: to state or announce

document: a formal piece of writing

draft: an early form of a document

militia: a group of people who only fight when needed

permanent: unable to be removed

perpetual: lasting forever

ratify: to give formal approval to something

rebellion: a fight to overthrow a government

representative: one who stands for a group of people

resolution: an official statement of purpose voted on by a group

FOR MORE INFORMATION

Books

Clay, Kathryn. *The U.S. Constitution: Introducing Primary Sources*. North Mankato, MN: Capstone Press, 2016.

Maloof, Torrey. *We the People: Founding Documents*. Huntington Beach, CA: Teacher Created Materials, 2017.

Websites

The Articles of Confederation
congressforkids.net/Independence_articles.htm
Review important information about this early US constitution.

INDEX